JR. GRAPHIC ENVIRONMEN

COLLISION
ASTEROID

J 523.44 Nel
Nelson, John
Collision course :
asteroids and Earth

$10.35
ocn183162467
05/28/2009

1st ed.

John Nelson

PowerKiDS press.

New York

Published in 2009 by The Rosen Publishing Group, Inc.
29 East 21st Street, New York, NY 10010

Copyright © 2009 by The Rosen Publishing Group, Inc.

All rights reserved. No part of this book may be reproduced in any form without permission in writing from the publisher, except by a reviewer.

First Edition

Editors: Joanne Randolph and Geeta Sobha
Book Design: Greg Tucker
Illustrations: Dheeraj Verma/Edge Entertainment

Library of Congress Cataloging-in-Publication Data

Nelson, John, 1960–
  Collision course : asteroids and Earth / John Nelson.
      p. cm. — (Jr. graphic environmental dangers)
  Includes index.
  ISBN 978-1-4042-4228-9 (lib. bdg.) ISBN 978-1-4042-4595-2 (pbk)
ISBN 978-1-4042-3980-7 (6-pack)
  1. Asteroids—Collisions with Earth—Environmental aspects—Juvenile literature.
2. Environmental disasters—Juvenile literature. I. Title.
  QB377.N45 2009
  523.44—dc22
                                                    2007049630

Manufactured in the United States of America

CONTENTS

INTRODUCTION

Asteroids are objects in space made mostly of rock. If a large asteroid were to hit Earth, it could cause major harm that would alter life on Earth. The Chicxulub Basin, in Mexico, was created by an asteroid **collision** about 65 million years ago. This collision is believed to have helped kill off the dinosaurs.

Though the possibility of such a large asteroid hitting Earth again is small, astronomers study the skies closely for asteroid activity. Are we on a collision course?

COLLISION COURSE
ASTEROIDS AND EARTH

AN ENORMOUS OBJECT SPEEDS THROUGH SPACE. IT TRAVELS MORE THAN 50,000 MILES PER HOUR (80,465 KM/H).

DIRECTLY IN ITS PATH IS **PLANET** EARTH, HOME TO OVER SIX BILLION PEOPLE.

WHAT IF THIS GIANT ASTEROID HIT OUR PLANET? COULD ENTIRE CONTINENTS BE WIPED CLEAN OF LIFE? HOW MANY MILLIONS OF PEOPLE WOULD DIE?

THE POSSIBILITY OF OUR PLANET BEING HIT BY AN ASTEROID IS VERY REAL. IT COULD HAPPEN ANY DAY. . . .

ASTEROIDS ARE SPACE ROCKS THAT **REVOLVE** AROUND THE SUN. OTHER OBJECTS IN SPACE THAT REVOLVE AROUND THE SUN INCLUDE PLANETS AND MOONS.

THE SUN'S **GRAVITY** KEEPS THESE OBJECTS REVOLVING AROUND IT IN PATHS, CALLED **ORBITS**.

MORE THAN 90 PERCENT OF THE **SOLAR SYSTEM'S** ASTEROIDS ARE IN THE MAIN BELT. THE MAIN BELT IS LOCATED BETWEEN THE ORBITS OF JUPITER AND MARS.

ASTEROIDS ARE MADE OF ROCK, METAL, OR A COMBINATION OF BOTH. THEY CAN BE AS SMALL AS A PEBBLE . . . OR A LOT LARGER.

THE LARGEST KNOWN ASTEROID IS CERES. IT IS AS LARGE AS THE STATE OF TEXAS AND HAS A SPOT ON IT THAT WAS PROBABLY FORMED WHEN ANOTHER ASTEROID HIT IT.

SCIENTISTS KNOW THAT LARGE ASTEROIDS HAVE HIT EARTH IN THE PAST.

WHAT THEY DON'T KNOW IS WHEN THE NEXT ASTEROID WILL STRIKE . . .

. . . AND WHAT WILL HAPPEN WHEN IT DOES.

UNITED NATIONS HEADQUARTERS, NEW YORK CITY. A GROUP OF WORLD LEADERS AND RESPECTED SCIENTISTS IS MEETING.

... MAKING THE QUESTION NOT IF BUT WHEN.

AND AS YOU WILL SEE IN THE FOLLOWING IMAGES, THE DANGERS ARE FAR TOO GREAT FOR THE WORLD TO DISREGARD.

SOME OF YOU WILL THINK THAT THESE IMAGES ARE NOTHING MORE THAN SIMPLE ENTERTAINMENT ...

... BUT THE PROSPECT OF EARTH'S DESTRUCTION BY AN ASTEROID IS NO LAUGHING MATTER!

"MORE THAN 65 MILLION YEARS AGO, AN ASTEROID THE SIZE OF A MOUNTAIN CRASHED INTO THE COASTLINE OF WHAT IS NOW MEXICO.

"MANY SCIENTISTS, INCLUDING MANY OF YOU HERE TODAY, BELIEVE THAT THE EFFECTS OF THE **IMPACT** KILLED OFF THE DINOSAURS.

"IN 1947, AN ASTEROID EXPLODED OVER SIBERIA, RUSSIA, BEFORE IT CRASHED. THE BLAST FLATTENED TREES FOR 18 MILES (29 KM) IN ALL DIRECTIONS.

"THOUSANDS OF REINDEER WERE KILLED. THE EXPLOSION WAS HEARD ALMOST 700 MILES (1,127 KM) AWAY!"

COME NOW, MR. SECRETARY, HOW MUCH FORCE COULD IT POSSIBLY TAKE TO KILL A FEW HELPLESS REINDEER?

THE ASTEROID THAT ENDED DINOSAUR LIFE ON EARTH STRUCK WITH THE FORCE OF FOUR MILLION **NUCLEAR BOMBS.**

SO WE'RE NOT JUST TALKING ABOUT THE LIVES OF REINDEER, MS. CHEN.

SCIENTISTS BELIEVE THERE ARE THREE POSSIBLE **SCENARIOS** THAT COULD OCCUR IF A LARGE ASTEROID COLLIDED WITH EARTH.

IN THE FIRST ONE, THE ASTEROID IS DISCOVERED IN TIME, AND SCIENTISTS ARE ABLE TO CHANGE ITS PATH.

"THE SECOND SCENARIO IS NOT AS HOPEFUL. IN THIS CASE, THE ASTEROID IS **DETECTED** TOO LATE FOR US TO STOP IT.

"THE THIRD AND FINAL SCENARIO IS THE GRIMMEST OF ALL. AN ASTEROID HITS EARTH WITHOUT ANY WARNING.

"IN THESE LAST TWO SCENARIOS, THE PEOPLE OF EARTH WOULD HAVE NO CHANCE TO PREPARE THEMSELVES. THE DEATH AND DESTRUCTION WOULD BE UNIMAGINABLE."

THIS IS ALL VERY DRAMATIC, MR. SECRETARY...

...BUT WOULDN'T THE PROTECTIVE LAYERS OF THE EARTH'S ATMOSPHERE BURN UP AN ASTEROID?

AND IF THEY DIDN'T, CHANCES ARE, THE ASTEROID WOULD LAND HARMLESSLY IN AN OCEAN. AFTER ALL, WE ALL KNOW THAT EARTH IS 70% WATER.

ANITA CHEN

YOU DON'T SEEM TO GET IT, MS. CHEN.

"IF AN ASTEROID OF THE SIZE WE'RE TALKING ABOUT PLUNGED INTO AN OCEAN, THE WATER WOULD IMMEDIATELY HEAT UP TO 100,000° F (55,538° C).

"THE POINT OF IMPACT IS CALLED GROUND ZERO. ALL SEA LIFE IN THE AREA WOULD BE BOILED AND DESTROYED IN SECONDS.

"WITHIN SECONDS, THE ENTIRE WORLD WILL ALSO SHAKE. THERE WILL BE DEAFENING SOUNDS AND A BLINDING LIGHT."

"A MIXTURE OF WATER, ASTEROID BITS, AND OCEAN BEDROCK WILL SHOOT OUT FROM GROUND ZERO. THEY WILL TRAVEL AT 25,000 MILES PER HOUR (40,234 KM/H)."

"AN IMMENSE FIREBALL WILL FORM FROM THE STEAM AND MELTING ROCK. IT WILL LASH OUT 1,000 MILES (1,609 KM) FROM GROUND ZERO. EVERYTHING IN ITS PATH WILL BE MELTED DOWN TO A BARE ROCK SURFACE."

"THE REAL HORROR BEGINS SOON AFTER THAT.

"THE AIR GETS HEATED TO ABOUT 3,000° F (1,649° C), CREATING WINDS AS STRONG AS A HURRICANE. FOR THE NEXT 20 HOURS, THE EARTH'S SURFACE WILL BE **RAVAGED** BY THESE WINDS.

"THE SHAKING OF THE PLANET WILL PRODUCE *TSUNAMIS* AS HIGH AS THE ROCKY MOUNTAINS.

"MANY ELEMENTS OF OUR SOCIETY WILL BE DESTROYED."

EXCUSE ME, SIR. AS BAD AS THAT ALL SEEMS, IN THE END THE WATERS WOULD GO DOWN.

MS. CHEN, THE WATER LEVEL WILL BECOME THE LEAST OF OUR PROBLEMS. LET ME EXPLAIN WHAT WILL HAPPEN NEXT.

"UPON IMPACT, TRILLIONS OF TINY ROCK PARTICLES, OR BITS, WILL SHOOT INTO THE SKY. THERE, THEY WILL FORM CLOUDS.

"WHEN THEY REACH THE UPPER PART OF OUR ATMOSPHERE, THEY WILL BLOCK OUT THE SUN. EARTH WILL BE IN COMPLETE DARKNESS.

"THE AIR 40 MILES (64 KM) UP WILL REACH 1,800° F (982° C), CAUSING EARTH'S TEMPERATURES TO REACH 600° F (316° C) FOR HOURS.

"SUCH HIGH TEMPERATURES WILL DESTROY ANY LIFE THAT IS UNABLE TO SHIELD ITSELF. ANYTHING THAT CAN BURN WILL DO SO INSTANTLY.

"SOOT FROM FIRES ALL OVER THE WORLD WILL RISE TOWARD THE SKY, CREATING *SMOG* OVER 17 MILES (27 KM) THICK.

"THE SMOG WILL MIX WITH AIRBORNE PARTICLES AND COVER ALL OF EARTH WITHIN 24 HOURS.

"THIS SMOG WILL LAST MONTHS, IF NOT YEARS. WITHOUT SUNLIGHT, MOST LIFE WILL CEASE TO EXIST. OUR AIR AND WATER WILL BECOME POISONED AND THE WATER DEADLY TO ALL WHO DRINK IT.

"RAIN WILL BEGIN TO FALL BUT NOT THE LIFE-GIVING WATERS WE THINK OF. THIS RAIN WILL HOLD TOXIC ACIDS, WHICH WILL DESTROY EARTH'S LIFE-FORMS.

"THE RAIN WILL WASH THE POISONS FROM ROCKS AND SOIL INTO RIVERS, PONDS, AND STREAMS, KILLING OFF ANY REMAINING LIFE THERE MAY BE IN THE WATER.

"THE EARTH WILL GROW COLD BECAUSE OF THE LACK OF SUNLIGHT. WITHIN 10 DAYS, THE PLANET WILL EXPERIENCE TEMPERATURES THAT ARE COLDER THAN THOSE OF ARCTIC WINTERS.

"SCIENTISTS HAVE TERMED THIS EFFECT IMPACT WINTER.

"THE FEW CREATURES THAT REMAIN ALIVE WILL NEED TO BE ABLE TO LIVE IN THESE CONDITIONS AND WITH NO FOOD. EVERYTHING ELSE WILL FREEZE OR DIE OF HUNGER.

"EVENTUALLY THE SMOG WILL BEGIN TO CLEAR AND SUNLIGHT WILL ONCE AGAIN REACH EARTH.

"EARTH'S ATMOSPHERE WILL NOW TRAP THE SUN'S HEAT INSTEAD OF LETTING IT OUT. THE IMPACT WINTER WILL BE FOLLOWED BY A STEAMY, HOT CLIMATE ALL OVER THE WORLD.

"THIS MAY LAST FOR A FEW MILLION YEARS."

"THE LIFE THAT WOULD EVENTUALLY APPEAR AFTER THE EVENTS I HAVE DESCRIBED WOULD BE QUITE DIFFERENT FROM ANYTHING ALIVE TODAY."

"ONE OPTION IS TO SEND A ROCKET WITH A NUCLEAR BOMB ON IT AT THE COMING ASTEROID.

"HOPEFULLY, THE BOMB WOULD SMASH THE ASTEROID INTO THOUSANDS OF SMALLER, HARMLESS PIECES.

"IF THE ASTEROID IS TOO LARGE TO DESTROY, THE BOMB COULD BE USED TO KNOCK THE ASTEROID OUT OF ITS ORBIT SO IT WOULD MISS EARTH.

"ANOTHER OPTION IS TO LAND A SPACECRAFT ON THE ASTEROID AND SECURE LARGE ROCKET ENGINES ONTO IT.

"ONCE THE ROCKET ENGINES WERE IN PLACE . . .

"THEY COULD THEN BE TURNED ON AND DIRECT THE ASTEROID OFF ITS COLLISION COURSE WITH EARTH.

"A LESS DRAMATIC WAY TO PROTECT OURSELVES FROM ASTEROIDS IS BY USING OUR OBSERVATORIES TO DETECT ASTEROIDS IN SPACE.

"BY HAVING OUR SCIENTISTS MONITOR OUR SKY FOR NEAR-EARTH OBJECTS, WE WILL HAVE LESS OF A CHANCE OF BEING SURPRISED BY AN ASTEROID.

"AMATEUR ASTRONOMERS ALSO PLAY AN IMPORTANT PART IN WATCHING FOR SIGNS OF ASTEROIDS. THEY CAN REPORT ANYTHING THEY FIND TO GOVERNMENT SPACE PROGRAMS."

ASTEROID FACTS

1. Ceres, the first recorded asteroid, was sighted by Giuseppi Piazzi in January 1801.

2. Asteroids range in sizes, from small dust particles to large bodies that are 600 miles (966 km) wide.

3. Asteroids that orbit close to Earth are called near-Earth asteroids, or NEAs.

4. Some asteroids have their own moons.

5. Asteroids are also known as minor planets.

6. The NEAR Shoemaker was the first spacecraft to land on an asteroid. It flew around the asteroid Eros for a year, then landed on it in February 2001.

7. Asteroids called binaries are found in pairs that revolve around each other.

8. In June 2007, the National Aeronautics and Space Administration (NASA) will launch *Dawn*, a spacecraft that will study two asteroids, Ceres and Vesta.

9. Jupiter's gravity keeps the asteroids in the Main Belt from colliding with Mercury, Venus, Earth, and Mars.

10. Asteroids are not globes, like planets, because they do not have enough gravity to pull them into that shape.

GLOSSARY

AMATEUR *(A-muh-tur)* Someone who does something without pay.

COLLISION *(kuh-LIH-zhun)* Two or more things hitting each other.

DETECTED *(dih-TEKT-ed)* Found out or discovered.

GRAVITY *(GRA-vih-tee)* The natural force that causes objects to move toward the center of a planet, like Earth, or other body.

IMPACT *(IM-pakt)* The hitting of one body against another.

NUCLEAR BOMBS *(NOO-klee-ur BOMZ)* Exploding weapons that use the energy found in the nucleus, or center, of an atom, which is the smallest bit of matter.

ORBITS *(OR-bits)* Circular paths.

PLANET *(PLA-net)* A large object, such as Earth, that moves around the Sun.

RAVAGED *(RA-vijd)* Destroyed something by using violence.

REVOLVE *(rih-VOLV)* To move around or to spin.

SCENARIOS *(se-NAR-ee-ohz)* Possible courses of events.

SMOG *(SMOG)* Pollution that hangs in the air.

SOLAR SYSTEM *(SOH-ler SIS-tem)* A group of planets that circles a star.

TSUNAMIS *(soo-NAH-meez)* Series of waves caused by movements in Earth's crust on the ocean floor.

Harris County Public Library
Houston, Texas

INDEX

WEB SITES

Due to the changing nature of Internet links, PowerKids Press has developed an online list of Web sites related to the subject of this book. This site is updated regularly. Please use this link to access the list:

www.powerkidslinks.com/ged/asteroid/